NATIONAL GEOGRAPHIC SOCIETY

DESTINATION:

RAIN FOREST

by Jonathan Grupper

SCHOLASTIC INC.

New York Toronto London Auckland Sydney
Mexico City New Delhi Hong Kong

The air is humming and heavy with moisture. Take a deep breath. Look around. In every direction, you can see only a few feet ahead, for you are closed off by a wall that's dense and green. And yet, you know that you're not alone. A thousand hidden eyes are upon you as you enter the tropical rain forest.

Rain Forest in Central America

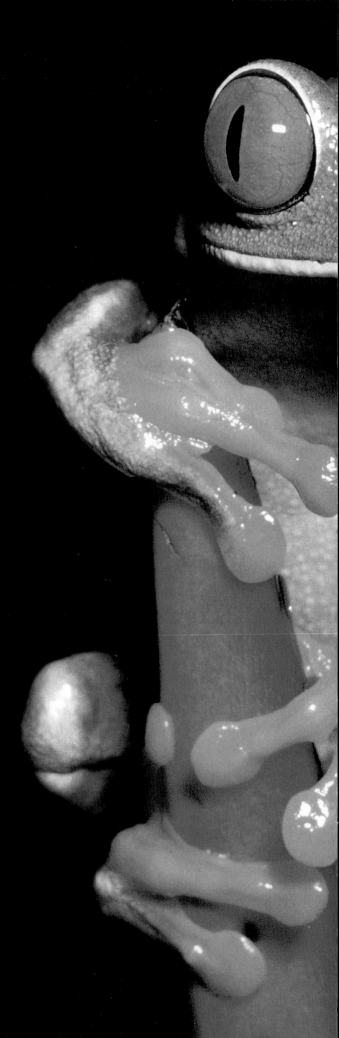

Look up—a howler monkey in the treetops lets out a loud call. Look right— a red-eyed tree frog springs onto a bright bromeliad leaf. Look around—every animal seems so different, because each has developed body parts and behaviors that help it survive in its own part of the rain forest.

Red-Eyed Tree Frog, Central America

The truth is, this is four worlds in one. From the ground up, there's the dark forest floor, the understory, the canopy, and the sunny emergent layer.

Each is like a separate neighborhood, inhabited by a separate set of creatures. Every level of life has staked out the place where the amount of sunlight best suits its needs.

Which layer would you choose to live in?

Emergent Layer

Toucan

The tallest trees form the emergent layer, which gets the most light, heat, and rain, and the toughest beating from the winds. Monkeys, birds, and insects swing, swoop, and flit here.

Canopy

Vine Snake

Beneath the giant trees spreads a second layer of trees whose rich, leafy branches interlock to form a "canopy." Rain filters through this level, soaking the branches and vines so that many turn into hanging gardens of orchids, bromeliads, and ferns. Creatures from tree frogs and crabs to snakes, sloths, and monkeys make highways across the thick branches—and find many hiding places.

Understory

Fruit Bat

Under the canopy trees grow the trees of the understory, such as strangler figs and coconut palms. Butterflies, lizards, bats, and snakes may roam here.

Forest Floor

Wasp

All day long, shadowy green twilight fills the forest floor. The air is still, humidity is high, and rivers are sluggish. You may find otters, rodents, snakes, ants, alligators, and wasps.
Central and South America (all)

It's four in the morning and the rain forest is still black with night. Turn on your flashlight and look near your feet. The forest floor is swarming with activity.

An army of seven million leafcutter ants is busily wrapping up its night's work, clearing the ground of five tons of leaves, one small scrap at a time. Imagine—if they were the same size as you, in the last eight hours they would have stripped an area as large as the state of Indiana!

Working together, they carry their precious load to their underground nest, which could be the size of a house. There, they mix the leaves with their saliva and droppings to grow a fungus that they eat.

vn, you'd
r be ready
ome action.
est erupts
ground of
rass is eaten
r ants who
an anole
s eaten by
iper who is
opical
who is eaten
called a tayra
by a jaguar.
end up
fungi and
their
o make food,
for the grass.

Eating Anole, Central and South America

It's called the food chain—which basically means that the big animal that eats the small one might end up becoming breakfast for the biggest of all. That's why it's so important that every species in the rain forest survives. Without one of them, many others will be affected, up and down the food chain.

t's still morning, but already the air is very hot. You crouch by a river to cool off—but don't dive in! Here come the piranhas. Each fish is only about as long as your foot, but a school of them can tear a victim to bits in seconds.

The water creatures around here are pretty wild: giant river otters, huge caiman alligators, and the world's largest snake—the anaconda.

Are you sure you still want to stand so close to the edge?

Anaconda, South America

Giant Otters and Caiman (CAY-mun), South America (below)

By noon, sunlight is filtering down through the leaves up above. You stare in amazement as a beautiful black, yellow, and red passion-vine butterfly flitters through the light beams to land on a red flower.

Animals and plants of the rain forest don't only eat each other. Sometimes they help one another to survive. It's taken thousands of years for this kind of butterfly to develop mouthparts that fit the blossom of the flower it's named after. The butterfly gets to eat, and the flower, in turn, gets its pollen spread when the butterfly moves on.

Passion-Vine Butterfly and Flower, South America

The swollen-thorn acacia tree is home for acacia ants that protect it from enemy insects.

Other tree-lovers include animals who share the same tree holes—opossums by day, monkeys by night. There are also 900 different species of wasp, each designed to pollinate a different species of fig tree!

Cooperation is often the law of the jungle.

Acacia Ant in a Swollen-Thorn Acacia Tree, South America

Agouti, South America

It's afternoon, the time when it's hottest, so most animals lie low. But when you least expect it, there's a sudden burst of activity in the understory. It's a jaguar, a kind of cat that's a lot larger and more ferocious than the cats you're used to. As it slips through the brush, an agouti, a large rodent, lets out a sharp whistle of alarm.

A macaw in the canopy heeds the agouti's warning and takes flight. The bird may return the favor by signaling the agouti the next time a predator swoops down from the sky.

Jaguar, Central and South America

Three-Toed Sloth, Central and South America

The canopy is a jungle gym of vines and branches. By late afternoon, spider monkeys are really making miles. This is the busiest layer of the rain forest, rich with creatures like sloths, vine snakes, orangutans, and opossums.

Hanging over your head is a remarkable plant called a bromeliad, which holds a miniature world of animals including poison-dart frogs and tiny crabs. They all gather in the small pool that collects where the leaves form a cup.

It's quiet again, and the spider monkeys have found a new patch of fruits and nuts to eat.

How would you like to take a swing through their treetops with them?

Bromeliad,
Central and South America

Crab and Poison-Dart Frog, Central and South America

Spider Monkey,
Central and South America

Strangler Fig,
Central and South America

Spider monkeys suddenly scramble for cover. Without any warning, sheets of rain pour down with unbelievable force. Hurry! You race for the shelter of a strangler fig. Its branches wrap around other trees, forming a thick cover.

Nearly every afternoon, the skies open up in a furious downpour. This is because the warm air of the forest rises to mix with the cool air above the treetops. In parts of the Amazon, more than ten feet of rain fall each year. In fact, the Amazon River, in South America, has more than two-thirds of the entire earth's flowing water.

While animals can find places out of the pounding rain, the ground has only leaves and roots to protect it from the storm. Look at your feet: Where there is no tree cover, the soil is simply being washed away. The rain forest is remarkably fragile.

Rain Forest, Central America

Rain Forest, Southeast Asia

The thunderstorm stops as suddenly as it began. But another sound replaces it: the roar of a chain saw. Run for cover! A tremendous tree is crashing down.

Every year, an area the size of Washington State is leveled. At this rate, there won't be any rain forests left in a century or so. Often, the reason for the destruction is that the people who live near a rain forest are unaware of its important resources, and cut down the trees to make farmlands.

Horned Toad, Southeast Asia

Flower Mantis, Southeast Asia

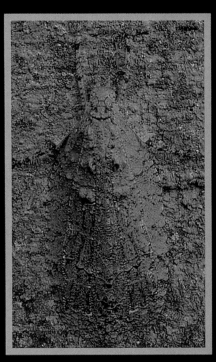
Gauzy Bush Cricket, Southeast Asia

Where the tree falls, the leaf litter seems to suddenly come alive, as insects that had been lying low now scatter every which way. Who would have guessed they were all hiding there?

Their way of staying concealed by blending in with their surroundings is called camouflage. It's another strategy for survival. Can you see these masters of disguise?

Of course, there are those who prefer life in the spotlight. The sun is beginning to set, and you peer up to see its last rays. Rising as high as a 20-story building, the tall treetops of the emergent layer crown the rain forest. There animals leap, swing, and glide among the trees.

This is a realm of color and flight: Some 2,600 kinds of birds—nearly a third of all bird species on earth—live in the rain forest. They range from the tiny hummingbird, which could fit inside your hand, to the fierce harpy eagle, earth's most powerful bird of prey, whose wingspan may be nearly twice your height. Some birds have beautiful plumage, designed to stand out against the forest greenery and attract the eye of a mate.

Hummingbird, Central and South America

Harpy Eagle, Central and South America

Tarsier, Southeast Asia

Night falls fast in the rain forest, and it gets darker here than anyplace you've probably seen. But it isn't bedtime, far from it. This is the hour when most creatures emerge. They are called nocturnal animals, and their senses are fine-tuned to detect both predators and prey in pitch black. Some relatives of the lemur, like the tarsier, are equipped with oversize eyes. Others, like the aye-aye, have a remarkable ability to hear or smell.

Want to know more about this wild place? Well, you could climb up a tree in a harness, or a hot-air blimp could drop you onto the heights in a tremendous rubber raft. You could stroll a walkway along the canopy to clip leaves of dozens of different plants for identification. Or how would you like to take a quick helicopter flight over the treetops to track some monkeys?

You could look for everything and anything— from new species to a cure for cancer. Today, scientists are going to great lengths to study this amazing tropical world— and slowly they're coming to know it from the forest floor all the way up to the emergent layer. Imagine what it would be like to be one of these students of the rain forest!

Rain Forest,
South America (both)

A Note from the National Geographic Society

The rain forest is an ancient greenhouse of life—it's also the richest and most diverse habitat on the planet. Because it's been around for millions of years, the plants and wildlife in it have had lots of time to develop in an incredible variety of ways and to form complex relationships. The examples you've seen in this book only hint at this richness. Most ra[in] forests are tropical, and grow in the warm, moist belt around the Equator. Only a few, called temperate rain forests, are in cooler part[s] of the world.

Gorilla, Africa

Of the roughly 10 million species of plants and animals on earth, perhaps 70 percent live i[n] tropical rain forests. In fact, we haven't even been able to identify most of them! A single tree might be home to more than 40 different kinds of plants. And one 25-acre area of Malaysian ra[in] forest, for instance, can hold more species of tre[es] than all of North America! In addition, anywhere between 5 and 30 million insect species may exist there.

To promote understanding of the plants, animals, and the habitat itself, National Geographic has funded the work of hundreds of research scientists, writers, and photographers in rain forests around the world since the beginning of the century. Studies range from poison-dart frogs to probing the canopy frontier.

Among earth's habitats, the rain forest is one of the least understo[od] and you can imagine why. Every square yard is like a separate mini-community—each with thousands of kinds of life-forms. There are hundreds of thousands of hidden plants and mosses, insects, and other organisms unknown to humans that may have vast contributions to make to medicine, the environment, and technology.

It's not just *what* plants and animals live in the rain forest, but *how* they survive, that is also a puzzle to scientists. The vines, mosses, and trees of this wet, humid, dense place grow with awesome speed. And as fast as they grow, they break down and return to feed the earth.

This is the rain forest's efficient way of recycling its nutrients —so efficient, in fact, that scientists have named rain forests the most productive vegetation systems on earth.

But rain forest plants couldn't survive, much less keep up an efficient lifestyle, if they weren't linked to the thousands of species of birds, mammals, reptiles, and insects that share their neighborhoods. Together plants and animals cooperate in various complex food chains. They depend upon one another to survive.

y-Tailed Opossum,
h America

Despite this vital interaction, there's a big factor that keeps rain forest systems from operating smoothly—or at all: people. Almost half of the tropical rain forest that once covered about six million square miles of the earth has been destroyed by humans. The rate of destruction between 1980 and 1990 alone was almost doubled from the previous decade. And as the human population grows, with its demands for rain forest land and products, threats to this precious ecosystem increase. The worst are logging, mining, pollution, and "slash-and-burn" methods to clear land for farms and cattle ranges.

-Aye, Africa

If destruction continues at this rate, what will happen? Climates all over the world will change violently and normal rainfall patterns will be altered; carbon dioxide in the atmosphere will increase to dangerous levels because forests will not be there to absorb it. Native peoples will be pushed from their ancient homelands, and still untapped resources for medicine and food will be lost forever.

Groups that wish to save the rain forest are finding ways for local people to support themselves—ways that aren't destructive, such as ecotourism or selective harvesting of fruits, nuts, and medicinal plants.

Some countries are taking a strong stand. For instance, India, Thailand, and the Philippines have declared their deforestation a national concern, and in Kenya and Colombia tree-planting movements are already making a difference.

Staff for this Book

Barbara Brownell,
Senior Editor

Jonathan Grupper,
Author

David Seager,
Art Director

Greta Arnold,
Illustrations Editor

Carl Mehler,
Map Editor

For Madeline and Jesse

ISBN 0-439-28701-4

12 11 10 9 8 7 6 5 4 3   2 3 4 5 6/0

Printed in the U.S.A.   14

First Scholastic printing, April 2001

National Geographic would like to thank Jim Dietz, Associate Professor of Zoology, University of Maryland, for reviewing the manuscript and illustrations and providing helpful comments.

FRONT COVER: A young scarlet macaw swoops through a rain forest in Peru, in South America.